SAND SCULPTURING

By Mickey Klar Marks

Photographs by Sidney G. Bernard

THE DIAL PRESS NEW YORK

For Edee Alberts and the Cape

17, 568

SAND SCULPTURING

Sand sculpture is fun to do and as easy to make as mud pies.

If you follow the simple step-by-step directions which are given in this book, you will get "molds" that make fine decorations. The only thing left to your imagination will be your own original design or composition. Everything else will be outlined for you, and the many photographs will show you exactly how a sand sculpture or a sand mold is made.

You can make any design that takes your fancy. Your tools are any object that you can lay your hands on. In fact your hands and fingers are tools as well.

You will find tools in the kitchen. For instance, you can use forks, spoons, glasses, potato mashers, etc. The sewing box is filled with tools: spools of thread, a darning egg, scissors, a thimble, and so on. The tool chest has screwdrivers, hammers, nails, pliers, etc. If you work in school, your tools may be pencils, compasses, paste pots, rulers, or the back of an old blackboard eraser. In other words, any object that has a form or shape is a "tool."

To make a sand sculpture, all you need are tools, a box of wet sand, and a bag of plaster.

All you have to do is to scoop or press your design into the wet sand and then cover the sand with plaster. In less time than it takes to make or bake a pie you can see your results. In a little more than an hour you have a piece of art ready to hang or display.

All your materials and tools should be at hand when you work. You also need a place to work. Any flat surface will do. At home or in the classroom you can use tables or desks or the drainboard on the kitchen sink. You also need water. The water is used to wet the sand and also to mix with the plaster that is used when the design is done.

If you are lucky enough to be at the seashore, you don't need a worktable. Then the work can be done right in the sand on the beach. More will be said about this later.

Sand belongs on a beach or in a fish tank or, in this case, in a box, not on the floor or in the soup. It is best to cover your work area with old newspapers or some covering so that the sand doesn't fly about or scatter. Plastic covers that come from the dry cleaners are useful. These make a good protective covering. There needn't be any sand in the scrambled eggs or any mess if you work carefully.

You will notice that there is no protective covering on the work area in the photographs that follow. The covering has been omitted here in order to be sure to give good, clear pictures.

MATERIALS

Sand, plaster, box, strong cord, bowl, old toothbrush or soft brush, water.

Any kind of sand will do for your sand sculpture. The next time you go to the beach you can bring home a boxful of it. If you cannot get beach sand, you can buy play sand at toy stores or in any pet shop.

There are many grades of sand, some fine, some coarse. You can use either. If you prefer a fine surface, use fine sand, which will give the sculpture a flat look. If you would rather have a rougher, more textured effect, you should use coarse sand.

Pet shops carry several grades for fish tanks. One pound of sand costs approximately eight cents. Four pounds of sand will fill an ordinary cigar box. You can re-use the sand for several molds since only a small amount of it sticks to the plaster when your sculpture is done.

Plaster can be bought in any hardware store. I use plaster of Paris. A five-pound bag sells for about thirty-two cents and five pounds will make at least four small molds (cigar or shoe box sizes).

Any box of any size or shape will do for your sculpture. I find cigar boxes best, for they are usually made of thin wood or heavy cardboard that give support to the mold and won't buckle when the plaster is poured. You can get cigar boxes from any cigar or drugstore. They are usually happy to save them and give them away. However, any cardboard box that isn't too flimsy will make a good mold. You can use shoe boxes, tie boxes, scarf boxes, and so on.

You need a strong piece of cord to be used for the "picture hook."

The bowl is needed for mixing plaster.

The soft brush is used for brushing excess sand from the sculpture after it has been "turned out."

TOOLS

Hands, fingers, spatulas, water glasses, jars, bottles, bottle tops, spoons, forks, figurines, etc. Rulers, compasses, pencils, paste pots, etc. Scissors, thimbles, spools of thread, etc. Hammer, pliers, screwdrivers, nails, etc. Any object that has shape or form.

There are some "extras" you can use in the sculptures. You may want to use shells, beads, stones, bits of wire, or wood in your design. For instance, to make a fish's eye, you can press a bead into the sand for the eye instead of pressing the shape of the eye into the sand with a tool.

Making a sand sculpture is really very simple.

STEP 1

Pour the sand into the box.

Fill the box with sand, leaving ½ inch of space at top of the box. This ½ inch is for your plaster backing.

STEP 2

Wet the sand thoroughly.

Mix the water and sand together. The sand must be wet but still firm. If the sand is too dry, it will not keep an impression. If the sand is too wet, your impressions will break down.

Always remember to work in firm sand, not *Dry*, not *Puddly*. But be sure the sand is saturated.

STEP 3

Level the sand by smoothing it with your hand or with a spatula or with a plasterer's scraper until you have an even surface.

STEP 4

Make the "picture hook."

Take a piece of cord and tie two strong knots, one on each end of it. If you are using a cigar box for the mold, you will need a piece of cord about two inches long. Put the picture hook aside until you are ready for it.

STEP 5

Have the bowl and the bag of plaster on the table ready to mix.

Have the tools on the table ready for use.

If you intend to use shells, beads, stones, bits of wire or wood as part of your design, have those at hand also.

Everything is ready but your idea for a composition. It is good to think out a design before starting your sculpture. If you can draw, make a sketch of your composition on a piece of paper, and then work it in the sand.

This isn't necessary, however. You don't have to know anything about drawing. You can work directly in the sand from an idea in your head. If you wish, you can experiment with various "tools." You can do several designs until you get one that pleases you. The nicest part of working in sand is that you can erase out any design until you have found one that you like. Then, pour the plaster and preserve your design.

It is a good idea to make your first mold an experiment. In this way you will learn to mix plaster and become familiar with the simple means of casting in the sand.

It is also important to remember not to press or dig too deeply into the sand. If you do dig to the bottom of the box, the plaster will run through and spoil the effect of your sculpture. Remember, you don't want a plaster cast, you want a sand cast.

14

HAND CAST

Press your own hand into the box of wet sand.

Make a deep impression of your hand. Remove your hand carefully so that the print is set firmly and clearly outlined.

Your design is ready. Now you will cast your design.

HOW TO MIX PLASTER

Pour water into a bowl.

Add plaster.

Never put plaster into bowl first for it will not mix properly.

You need about ⅓ more plaster than water. If you use 3 cups of water, you will need 4 to 4½ cups of plaster. Your mixture is ready when the plaster and water look and feel like heavy cream.

This cigar box used for the hand cast measures 2½ inches high, 6½ inches wide, 8 inches long.

For this size box we use 2 measuring cups of water and 2½ to 3 cups of plaster.

(If the mixture is too thin, add a little more plaster until you get the "heavy cream.")

15

Stir the water and plaster at once and be sure there are no lumps in the mixture. Plaster must be used at once, for it sets fast.

If your plaster gets too thick and starts to harden, throw it away, for it will not pour. You cannot thin the plaster with water. Start fresh and make a new batch.

Take a small amount of plaster and carefully dribble it onto your sand design. Dribble the plaster into the deeper impressions first, then cover the rest of the surface of sand with plaster.

Never pour your plaster directly from the bowl. Plaster is heavy and will break down the impressions you have made if you do not dribble the first layer into those impressions carefully at first.

When you have covered your design with a thin first layer of plaster (make sure all the impressions are

filled), you may then pour the rest of the plaster from the bowl into the box, until the plaster fills the ½ inch space you have allowed for your backing.

Level the plaster so that you have a flat backing.

Level it with a spatula, plasterer's tool, or your own hand.

If you haven't mixed enough plaster to fill your mold, don't worry. As long as you have covered your design with the first layer, you can mix another batch of plaster and pour it into your mold.

While the plaster is still soft, carefully place the knotted cord or "picture hook" into the plaster. Center the cord so that when your mold is turned out, the sculpture will hang straight. Do not dig the cord too deeply into the plaster for you might break through to your sand design.

It takes approximately one hour for a small mold to set. The plaster will harden almost immediately and will feel cold to the touch. In about a half-hour the plaster feels warm. Then it turns cold once again. In an hour you can "turn out" your mold.

Pry off one side of the box. If you are using a cardboard box, you can peel off one side.

Now pry off the other three sides of the box.

Carefully lift your mold out. Turn it over and place it on the table.

Don't be disappointed if all you see is a square of wet sand. Let your mold dry for another half-hour.

Most of the sand you have used will remain in the bottom of the box from which you have removed the sides. Since the sand was saturated, it will not crumble or fall away. Any sand that does scatter will land on the paper, table, or protective covering and can be

18

cleaned when you are through working. The sand can be used again. Place the remaining sand into a box for future use.

Your sand sculpture is now dry enough for you to brush. Gently brush the surface to remove excess sand. This sand isn't sticking to your plaster backing. As you brush, your design will begin to appear.

Sand sculpture actually consists of nine parts plaster to one part sand. Only a small amount of sand sticks to the plaster.

After you have brushed your mold a few times, you will notice that only a few grains will come off. You have brushed enough and your sand sculpture is finished. Don't be alarmed if sand keeps falling when you touch your sculpture. You won't miss those grains, and after a while when the mold is thoroughly dried out, not a grain will fall.

Although your sculpture is finished, it is wise to let it dry out for several days before hanging. The plaster will then dry out thoroughly. Your mold will become much lighter in weight when all the moisture from the plaster has evaporated. You will also notice that the sand will lighten in color and take on its permanent value.

You have made your first sculpture. It was an exercise, just for fun. It was an exercise to make you familiar with your materials. You might want to save the first mold of your hand just as the famous movie stars do. But let us consider it an exercise.

You are now ready to do a simple sand sculpture.

FLOWER POT

Tools: Paste jar or cold cream jar, pencil or nail, top of ink bottle or bottle cap, box (any small box will do).

STEP 1

Press the jar into the wet sand.

Dig the top portion of the jar deeper into the sand than the lower portion.

STEP 2

Make a curved line with the pencil or nail for the stalk.

STEP 3

Press the top of the bottle cap into the sand to make the flower petals.

STEP 4

Use the open or screw-end of the bottle cap to make the center of the flower.

STEP 5

Draw leaves with the pencil or nail, digging gently into the sand.

STEP 6

Mix the plaster, dribble and pour it, then place your hook. Let the cast dry, turn it out and brush.

With the same basic design you can get many different and interesting sculptures.

For instance, instead of using a bottle cap to make the flower petals, you can use shells or bits of colored glass. Press the shells or bits of glass into the wet sand. Don't press them in too deeply.

In this photograph colored bits of glass were used that had been found on the beach. The sea had smoothed and polished them.

Each one of you can have an original sculpture using the same basic design or the same model.

THE HOUSE

Tools: Wood block, ruler, small square bottle or square of wood, box.

STEP 1

Press the wood block into the sand, leaving ½ inch of space at the bottom edge of the box. Hold the wood block vertically and make four imprints, one right next to each other. Be sure your imprints are even in depth. Now make one deeper impression on the right-hand side of the first impression.

STEP 2

Leave ½ inch of space above the bottom impression. Turn the wood block (as shown in the photograph) and press it into the sand evenly, one right next to the other.

24

STEP 3

Press a bottle or wood square into the sand in the center of the box above the other imprints. Use the same small square to make an impression in the left-hand corner of the bottom, or first, impression.

STEP 4

Using your ruler, dig two lines above the square to form a V. Dig two short lines into the sand above the right-hand line.

STEP 5

Dig several straight lines with a pencil into the center impression.

Mix the plaster, dribble and pour it, then place your hook. Let the cast dry, turn it out and brush.

Here is another sculpture, using a twig and a miniature wood bird.

BIRD IN TREE

Tools: Nail file, twig from bush, hedge, or tree, small wooden bird, box.

STEP 1

Place the twig so that it looks like the trunk of a tree. Press gently into the wet sand.

STEP 2

With the point of a nail file dig into the sand to make the leaves of the tree. Don't dig too deeply.

STEP 3

Place the wooden bird on the branch. Press into sand. Make a line for the horizon with the point of the nail file.

Mix the plaster, dribble and pour it, then place your hook. Let the cast dry, turn it out and brush.

Any object that has shape or form will make an impression in wet sand. If you have a favorite little figurine—a china dog, a bronze cat, or a wooden doll—that you would like to use for a mold, you can do so. Here is a sand sculpture in which a pottery horse was used for the design.

HORSES
Tools: Pottery horse, pencil, box.

STEP 1

Press the head of the pottery horse into the wet sand on one side of the box. Repeat this twice, making one impression deeper than the other two.

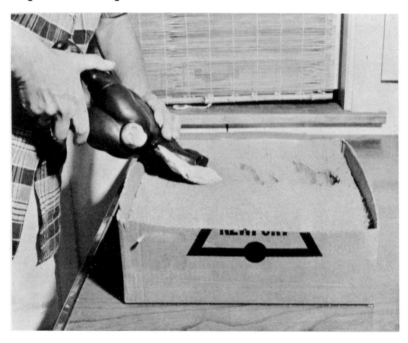

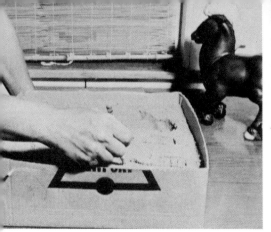

STEP 2

Using the pencil, make letters that are similar to ancient writing—Egyptian or Persian or Chinese. Draw these letters on the other side of your sculpture, being sure not to dig too deeply.

Mix the plaster, dribble and pour it, then place your hook. Let the cast dry, turn it out and brush.

This sand sculpture looks like an old fragment you might find in a museum.

29

Some of the most interesting sculptures are abstracts. These are designs or compositions that do not necessarily depict anything realistic. They are interesting because they have form, composition, and varying depths that give light and dark effects.

In sand sculpture you can scoop out sand to make your design. Instead of pressing a tool into the wet sand, you scoop the sand out. The following simple abstract will show you how to scoop a design.

ABSTRACT

Tools: Small spatula or plasterer's scraper, small glass or small jam jar, box.

STEP 1

Scoop out an area in the upper left-hand corner. Be sure your edges are clean and straight.

STEP 2

Scoop out an area on the left-hand side of the box. This should be deeper than the area in Step 1.

STEP 3

Scoop out the sand on the right-hand side of the box directly opposite the area of Step 2.

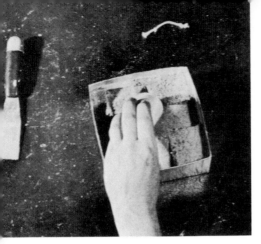
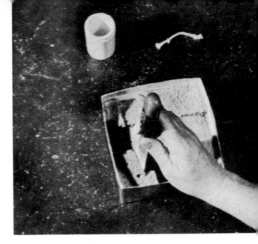

STEP 4

Scoop out the sand at the bottom of the box.

STEP 5

Press the bottom of a small glass or jar to make semicircles in the center of the box. Press first impression deeper than next two.

STEP 6

With your spatula make a cross in the bottom, right-hand corner of the sand. Dig two lines in the bottom, left-hand corner.

Mix the plaster, dribble and pour it, then place your hook. Let the cast dry, turn it out and brush.

Have you remembered to insert your picture hook? You didn't? Well, don't worry. Your sand sculpture can be displayed resting on a plate stand. You can buy a plate stand made of wire in a five-and ten-cent store, or in hardware stores or gift shops.

You may also mount your sculpture on a piece of wood. Simply put two hooks and a picture wire on the back of the wood and then glue the sculpture to the front of the wood.

In the beginning of this book I promised to tell you how to do sand sculpture at the beach. You do not need a worktable at the beach. You work directly in the sand. Instead of using a box for your mold, all you need are four pieces of wood—driftwood or any old wood you can find to make your mold. Your materials are the same. You need sand, and you have miles of it all around you. You need plaster, a pail or bucket, a piece of cord, a brush, and water. You have an oceanful of the last item. Your tools may be beach toys, wood, shells, a shovel, rocks, your hands and feet. Again, anything that will make an impression in wet sand.

The sculptures are made exactly the same way that you make them at home or at school. The one main difference is that you do not have to worry about digging too deeply. You can dig your design as deeply as you wish, and you will get some exciting effects.

Your mold is exactly as it is at home or at school. However, if the day is bright and sunny (and it generally is when one spends a day at the beach), your mold will be ready to turn out in fifteen or twenty minutes. In turning out your mold, instead of breaking or peeling your box away from the mold, all you do is carefully lift out one piece of wood at a time. Turn out your mold. Let it dry for ten minutes and then brush.

In doing more advanced work, whether at the beach, home, or at school, the method is always the same. Just press or scoop in wet sand to get your design.

Have you noticed that when you dig a line in the sand on the left-hand side of the box, the line appears on the right-hand side when your mold has been cast and turned out. That is because you are always doing your design in reverse.

For instance, if you want to sign your sculpture and your name is Jean, you would have to write your letters backwards like this: *ᘉɒɘſ* Write your name on a slip of paper and look at it in a mirror and that is what you would see.

When you are ready to do a more advanced sand sculpture and you have decided on your composition or sketched a design for your composition on paper,

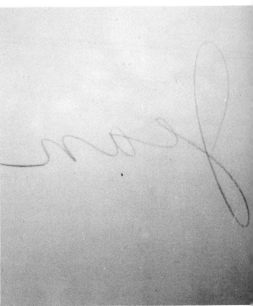

you must remember to work in reverse. That is, if you want a square, for example, to appear on the right-hand corner of your sculpture, you must scoop or press it in on the left corner. If you have a stone or a shell that you want to be in the left-hand corner of your sculpture, you must place it in the right-hand corner as you work.

Varying the depths in your sculpture will give you better effects. You will have more "interest" in your piece, more lights and shadows. Your composition will have character and not be just a dull plaque.

Here are photographs of two sculptures. One is shallow, and one has depths and shallows, hills and valleys. The second sculpture is the "stronger" of the two.

In doing larger pieces we follow the same simple directions as for small pieces. We choose a larger box, we impress our design as we did for the small molds, and we mix our plaster in the same way. There is one important difference in pouring our plaster. After dribbling the first layer from our fingers onto the sand, take pieces of florist wire and place it on the plaster. Then pour the remaining plaster over the crisscrossed wire reinforcement.

The wire reinforces the mold so that it will be strong and not break when it is turned out. Small molds can be reinforced in the same fashion for extra strength. Chicken mesh can be used in place of florist wire.

When making the "picture hook" for the large sand sculptures, wrap a piece of florist wire around the cord for extra strength.

The large sculpture can also be mounted on a block of wood by gluing it to a wooden board with any strong adhesive product.

The following are photographs of small and large pieces that I have done. The same ready-to-find tools were used in making them. The only bought tool is a plasterer's scraper, which can be bought cheaply in any paint shop.

The world is as full of objects as ideas. You can make sand sculptures that are not only exciting and decorative but artistic as well. Sand sculpture is an old and simple art form, but it is an art nonetheless. Perhaps you won't turn out museum pieces, but you can turn out molds that will make any room more attractive.

You are on your own. The door is open.